In Heaven I Will

Storyline **Pamela Consuegra**
Illustrations **Rob Harrell**

I can't walk now.

But in heaven,
I will hike all day.

I can't talk now.

But in heaven,
I will sing songs.

I can't hear now.

But in heaven,
I will hear angels sing.

I can't see now.

But in heaven,
I will see Jesus' face.

I can't swim now.

But in heaven,
I will swim with dolphins.

I can't run now.

But in heaven,
I will run fast.

I can't climb now.

But in heaven,
I will climb a tall tree.

In heaven, all will
be made new.